The Brief History of World War 1

The Great War, Western and Eastern Front Battles, Chemical Warfare, and how Germany Lost, Leading to the Treaty of Versailles

(1914-1919)

Disclaimer

A quick overview

World War I, also called the **World War** or the **Great War**, was a world war that began in Europe on July 28, 1914 and lasted until November 11, 1918. November 11 remained known as Armistice Day.

All the major powers of the world were involved in this war and were composed of two conflicting alliances: the Allies (centered around the Triple Entente of the United Kingdom, France and Russia) and the Centrals (originally centered around the Triple Alliance of Germany, Austria-Hungary and Italy). These alliances reorganized (Italy defected to the Allies in 1915) and expanded as more countries joined the war (Romania joined the Allies and the Ottoman Empire and Bulgaria joined the Centrals).

In the end, more than 70 million soldiers, including 60 million Europeans out of a population of 460 million, were mobilized in one of the largest wars in history.

More than 9 million soldiers (13%) were killed, mainly as a result of great technological advances in firepower (it was the first war in which factory-made and rapidly produced means and technology prevailed, such as machine guns, poison gas, cannons and barbed wire, and in which tanks and airplanes came into general use) without corresponding developments in mobility (the tactics used still dated back to the 19th century and that, according to polemologists, was one of the causes of the huge numbers of killed (more than 16 million) and wounded (more than 21 million wounded soldiers (30%)).

Another important factor which also contributed to the massive sacrifice of human life was the possibility of

3

constantly calling up successive waves of thousands of young men as conscripts for several years in a row, taking them to the front and deploying them there.

This deployment became notorious mainly because, due to outdated tactics, often only futile successes could be reported, despite the sacrifice of very large numbers of soldiers.

This manifested itself in the capture of small pieces of mostly destroyed no man's land, which then had to be defended or recaptured over and over again with equally massive counterattacks, the so-called 'war of positions'.

It was the sixth deadliest conflict in world history, which subsequently paved the way for political reforms and/or revolutions in the countries concerned. In France (population 41 million in 1914) an estimated 4.3% of the population died, in United Kingdom 2.1% (out of 43 million inhabitants), in Germany (67 million inhabitants) 3.8%, in the Austro-Hungarian monarchy 3.7% (out of 51 million inhabitants), in the Ottoman Empire (with a population of 18.5 million) 14.5%, in the Russian Empire 1.7% (out of 166 million inhabitants).

On July 28, the conflict began with the Austro-Hungarian invasion of Serbia, followed by the German attack on France through Belgium and Luxembourg and a Russian attack on Germany. After the German advance on Paris came to a halt, the Western Front settled into a static war of attrition of trench warfare that changed little until 1917.

In the east, the Russian army fought successfully against the Austro-Hungarian troops, but was pushed back by the German army. Additional fronts were opened after the Ottoman Empire joined the war in 1914, Italy and Bulgaria in 1915 and Romania in 1916.

The Russian Empire went down in the Russian Revolution of 1917, and Russia exited the war after the October Revolution later that year. After a German offensive along the Western Front in 1918, American troops entered the trenches, and the Allies forced the German armies back in a series of successful offensives.

Germany, which had its own problems with revolutionaries at the time (the November Revolution), agreed to a ceasefire on November 11, 1918, which would later be known as Armistice Day. The war ended as a victory for the Allies.

By the end of the war, four of the imperialist powers - the German, Russian, Austro-Hungarian and Ottoman empires - had been defeated militarily and politically: the successor states of the first two lost much territory, while the last two ceased to exist altogether.

From the Russian Empire the revolutionary Soviet Union arose, while in Central Europe all kinds of new small states were formed. The League of Nations was founded in the hope of preventing such a conflict in the future.

But out of this war came European nationalism and the disintegration of former empires. The consequences of Germany's defeat and the Treaty of Versailles would eventually contribute to the outbreak of World War II in 1939.

The First World War was mainly fought in Europe. The term 'World War' refers to the many English and French troops that were brought to Europe from the colonies, but also to the battles that actually took place in colonies such as Africa, the Pacific and the Middle East.

6

However, the scale of this extra-European battle was dwarfed by the massiveness and intensity of the fighting in Europe itself.

After three years of war (in 1917), the Centrals were almost exhausted. But so were the Allied French, Russians, British and Italians. In that year, the United States joined the battle and in the end, this victory was decisive for the Allies.

After the Crown Prince of Austria-Hungary Franz Ferdinand and his wife Countess Sophie Chotek were shot dead by Bosnian Serb nationalist Gavrilo Princip in Sarajevo on 28 June 1914, Emperor Franz Joseph of Austria-Hungary, with the support of his ally the German Empire, proposed the July ultimatum to Serbia.

When Serbia, supported by an alliance with Tsarist Russia, did not accept this ultimatum on all points, Austria-Hungary mobilized its armies and declared war on Serbia on 28 July. This set off a chain reaction: several existing military treaties came into effect, other states allied with either Austria-Hungary or Serbia also mobilized and declared war

7

on the opposing states eventually involving most European states in the conflict.

The war was between the Central Powers, led by Germany, and the Triple Entente which consisted of France, the United Kingdom and the Russian Empire. Italy, which had a treaty with Germany, adopted a neutral position because it did not agree with German plans concerning the Balkans. Neutral Belgium was invaded after a German ultimatum.

The war became a world war because of the British participation. The Ottoman Empire joined the Centrals, making the Middle East a battleground as well.

As a static war with trenches was being fought in the west, Germany tried to force a decision at sea.

Thus the U-boat campaign became important because the United Kingdom depended on imports of goods and food. Unrestricted submarine warfare was first introduced in 1915. This was temporarily halted after the sinking of the Lusitania.

From 1914 to 1917 the borders of the western front hardly shifted. The battle was mainly characterised by bloody offensives that gained little ground.

Examples are the battle of Verdun and the battle of the Somme, which cost more than a million lives. This was partly because few innovative tactics were used.

In 1917 riots and disturbances broke out in the Russian Empire and a revolution followed. At the end of that year, in the October Revolution, the Romanov regime was overthrown and the Bolsheviks founded the Soviet Union.

Fighting against the Communists continued and Lenin signed a peace treaty, called Peace of Brest-Litovsk, with the Germans in early 1918. That same year, after the reintroduction of the unlimited submarine war and the Zimmermann telegram, the United States entered the war and shipped at least 25.000 new soldiers every month to France and Belgium. At sea, the German Empire was slowly but surely pushed back with new convoy tactics.

Table of Contents

11

Causes and trigger

The direct cause was the aforementioned murder of Franz Ferdinand and his wife Sophie Chotek. But the real causes lay deeper. Some historians see the growing popularity of militarism and radical nationalism in Europe as the cause.

These movements blamed their governments for passivity in the face of external threats, thus stimulating the arms race in 1912 and 1913. Other analyses blame imperialism, economic problems and the restless territorial expansion of the great powers.

Exceptional are the analyses that largely see the war as an initiative of the ruling class to curb a socialist revolution of the proletariat.

The long-running cause of the war was the imperialist foreign policy of most European nations, including the British Empire, France, the German Empire, the Austro-Hungarian Empire, the Ottoman Empire, the Russian Empire, Italy, and Serbia.

The mutual tension and rivalry had been slowly rising to boiling point for decades and it was finally waiting for a direct confrontation between the great powers. The murder of Franz Ferdinand and his wife resulted in a Habsburg ultimatum to Serbia, the so-called "July ultimatum".

Various alliances that had been formed during the preceding decades were invoked, so that within a few weeks the great powers were at war. Through their colonies, the conflict quickly spread around the world.

At the beginning of the 20th century, a shaky balance of power developed in Europe. Strong nationalistic movements emerged in several countries. France had lost Alsace-Lorraine to Germany after the Franco-Prussian War of 1870 and wanted to regain this territory.

It faced a united and therefore militarily strong Germany and made an alliance with Russia. At the beginning of the 20th century a new type of warship emerged: the Dreadnought. The United Kingdom and other countries had to rebuild their fleets. Germany took advantage of this by increasing its investments in the navy and wanted to acquire more military power at sea. This greatly worried the British, who saw their hegemony at sea threatened.

13

Thus Germany and the United Kingdom became involved in the German-British fleet race.

Under Otto von Bismarck's Realpolitik, Germany had been cautious in international diplomacy. Germany played countries diplomatically against each other, like at the Congress of Berlin. Only when a country stood alone diplomatically and had no strong allies who could intervene, war was waged. Afterwards, efforts were made to make peace for the defeated country as light as possible so that there would be no lingering resentments.

This was abandoned after the Franco-German War and especially the resignation of Bismarck. Under Kaiser Wilhelm II a more aggressive political policy was pursued: the Weltpolitik. This however alienated many states, which feared to see their own power threatened.

Germany and Austria-Hungary were allies and France had formed an alliance with Russia. After the Second Boer War England was looking for allies, but an English rapprochement with Germany was rejected by the Germans. England now sought rapprochement with France and Russia.

14

This alliance was then called the Triple Entente. Because of this, the German nation saw itself as the victim of a conspiracy directed against it. The Germans were also worried about the rapid Russian recovery after the defeat against Japan in 1905 and the subsequent revolutionary unrest.

At the same time, powerful nationalist ambitions blossomed in the Balkan states, seeking diplomatic support in Berlin and Vienna on the one hand and St. Petersburg on the other. The panslavists wanted Russian support for the Slavic peoples under Austrian rule.

In areas such as Slovenia, Silesia and Bohemia, a strong Slavic nationalist consciousness emerged, which in turn aroused fear and enmity among the Germans. The first pan-Germanic and anti-Semitic movements emerged (the seeds of National Socialism were sown in the 19th century).

Nationalists increasingly determined the policies of a government. More and more claims were being made and peoples who had lived under a different government for years and had adapted to it, such as the Czechs and

Poles, now wanted their own state. They increasingly sought support from extreme groups, such as the Black Hand in Serbia.

In contrast with France and the United Kingdom, Germany possessed few colonies, as a result of which this state was less seen as a great power. According to the then prevailing opinion in Germany, the great advantage of colonies lay in the control of trade flows and the privileged access to raw materials and markets. The Germans themselves saw it as a "disadvantage". Germany was the latecomer, to whom no "place under the sun" was granted.

Germany had the strongest army in the world; Germans generally believed that a possible war had to end in a German victory. Most nationalist groups therefore hoped for a conflict, and even those who did not want one did not feel the need to avoid war per se.

This picture was also seen in other countries. The French, for instance, would not have started a war themselves to regain Alsace-Lorraine, but they seized the excuse offered by Germany eagerly and went to war.

War was generally romanticized and, particularly by right-wing and nationalist groups across Europe, seen as 'the great purifier'. War made a person 'better, stronger, smarter and more mature', 'turned boys into men'. Issues that were referred to as 'social ills' (e.g. unemployment, socialism, feminism and homosexuality) would 'automatically dissolve' through war, thus once again securing the self-interest of all national elites. And after the (obviously won) war would come a golden age in which hegemony was secured, the economy would recover and grow, any territorial and colonial gains would provide new career opportunities, and the victorious soldiers would return home in grand triumphal parades.

The various alliances were weak. Both Germany and Russia, the stronger parties, allowed themselves to be led by their respective weaker allies Austria-Hungary and Serbia for fear of losing them.

Prior to the First World War, the various great powers drew up plans to "strike the first blow". In France, the extremely offensive Plan XVII was designed. In Germany, the Schlieffenplan was drawn up.

In Russia, the army plan was drawn up to immediately occupy East Prussia and advance on Berlin. To deal this first blow, mobilization of the armies was necessary. Mobilizations took time and could not be carried out in secret. In practice, this meant that a mobilization had to be immediately followed by a declaration of war; every day's wait meant an opportunity for the other side to mobilize as well. Both soldiers and politicians were aware of this.

Austria-Hungary was seriously weakened. The Dual Monarchy had been humiliated by Italy and Prussia, and it had been almost split in two by the Ausgleich of 1867; it now sought compensation through the Balkans. By the annexation of Bosnia and Herzegovina in 1908 it had recovered somewhat.

An easy victory over Serbia would allow Austria-Hungary to prove that it was still a great power. Bulgaria also felt humiliated and inadequate after the Balkan wars. Any chance to deal with Serbia, Romania and Greece was most welcome.

The Ottoman Empire had slowly lost more and more ground to the United Kingdom and France in Africa and to

Russia in the Caucasus in the decades leading up to the war.

In addition, almost the entire Ottoman province of Rumania (the Balkans) had gained independence from the Empire through Russian support in the Balkan Wars. These lost wars brought with them a huge influx of refugees; millions of Turks from the Balkans, Crimea and Caucasus settled in Central Anatolia. Germany, on the other hand, had never occupied Ottoman territory and supported the Ottoman government because of German investment in the Empire. The Ottoman Empire eventually plunged into World War I on the German side, primarily to regain lost territories in the Caucasus and Crimea from Russia and to prevent further loss of territory in the west.

However, increasing ethnic tensions in the multicultural empire had convinced the sultan and his government that the Ottoman Empire had to become more explicitly Turkish and that connections had to be sought with the other Turkish peoples in the Caucasus and Central Asia. These could join the fight against the Russians, who were also their enemy.

19

Some countries, such as Italy and Romania, were willing to go with the highest bidding side. This contributed to an expansion of the war.

Between 1900 and 1914 the various armies had been greatly modernized in terms of artillery and other weaponry. Also the organization was much improved to Prussian/German example of General Staff.

This did not apply to the plans and tactics. These were based on assumptions and misjudgements.

The start of the war

On 28 June 1914, the Austrian Archduke and heir to the throne Franz Ferdinand and his wife visited Sarajevo, the capital of the Austro-Hungarian province of Bosnia and Herzegovina.

The Bosnian Serbian student Gavrilo Princip shot French Ferdinand with a pistol, after another member of the Serbian gang of 'The Black Hand' had made an unsuccessful attempt to murder the crown prince and his wife with a grenade earlier that day. In that attempt only Ferdinand's officer was hit.

When Frans Ferdinand wanted to visit his officer in hospital, he and his wife were shot dead on the way.

Public opinion in Europe sided with Vienna and not with Serbia. Even the Russians withdrew their hands from the Serbs, their traditional allies. The attack seemed at first to end with a hiss: Austria did not seem to react.

Snowball

After the attack on 28 June, things remained seemingly quiet for several weeks. Behind the scenes, Vienna consulted successfully with Berlin. Berlin almost gave Vienna a blank cheque on 6 July, because the alliance between the two was defensive in character. This blank cheque consisted of the German promise that a Russian intervention would mean a German response.

It was only on 23 July that Vienna issued Serbia, through its Foreign Minister Count Leopold Berchtold, with a 48-hour ultimatum, the *July ultimatum*. This ultimatum demanded that the matter be got to the bottom of. For this, Serbia had to submit to a thorough violation of its sovereignty, including the admission of Austrian police officers.

Serbia also had to take responsibility for the attack. Serbia agreed to all but one of the demands, namely the admission of Austrian agents on its territory. Serbia regarded this as an infringement of its sovereignty and declared a partial mobilisation of its army.

Austria declared the response unsatisfactory and broke off diplomatic relations with Serbia on 25 July. Austria also declared a partial mobilisation. On 25 July, at the Krasnoje Selo crown meeting, Russia decided to provide military support to Serbia.

At the same time, a mediation conference was proposed by Russia, Germany and the United Kingdom. However, this proposal remained unanswered. A first phase in the mobilization of the Russian army followed on July 27. The commander of the Russian army, Sergei Dobrorolski, later said that the Russian staff considered the war a foregone conclusion already on July 25. It was known to them that Germany would follow this move.

On 26 July Germany decided not to go along with Russia's idea of military support and Austria intended to wage a local war, in part because the Serbian capital of Belgrade lay just across the border from Austria-Hungary. On July 28 Austria declared war on its small neighbor. The very next day, 29 July, Belgrade was shelled by Austrian artillery.

Austria-Hungary decided on 30 July to proceed with a general mobilisation. On the same day Tsar Nicholas II of Russia also approved the mobilization of the Russian army.

The Russian general staff, realizing that this implied an indirect declaration of war, tried to dissuade him. Also a letter of incantation from the German emperor to his cousin the czar remained ineffective. Germany set a 12-hour ultimatum; the Russian mobilization had to be withdrawn.

When there was no answer, Germany declared war on Russia on August 1. France also decided to mobilise in order to keep its alliance with Russia.

The German war plan was an updated version of the so-called Schlieffen Plan. This was based on the assumption that the Russian mobilization would take a long time. Germany would use this time to first deal with arch-enemy France and then deal with Russia. However, on the evening of the declaration of war, the first Russian units entered East Prussia.

The Schlieffen Plan provided for a circumvention movement through Belgium. On August 1, Germany occupied Luxembourg. On 2 August, Germany sent Belgium an ultimatum demanding free passage. Belgium refused the German troops passage and Germany declared war on neutral Belgium.

On August 3, Germany declared war on France, and on August 4, Germany entered Belgium. This was reason for the United Kingdom to declare war on Germany the same day, since the United Kingdom had guaranteed the neutrality of Belgium in the Treaty of London. With this last

25

British declaration of war, all European great powers were at war within one week.

Fronts of the First World War

European Fronts

- Western Front - The invasion of the German Empire in Belgium, Luxembourg and France. Here the trenches were used after the Germans stopped before Paris. After the advance of the Germans stopped, both sides tried to reach the sea as quickly as possible at a position favorable to them. This was also called the Race to the Sea.
- Eastern Front - The Russians invaded East Prussia here and caused a surprise. Yet the Germans and Austrians drove the Russians back to their own country.
- Balkan Front - The Austrians invaded Serbia with the support of the Germans. Later other countries such as Romania, Montenegro, Bulgaria and Greece were also involved in the war.
- Italian Front - The Italians joined the Allies in 1915 after being promised much if the war was won. The Italians thought they could beat the Austrians but even here the battle kept going back and forth.

Only at the end were the Allies able to force a breakthrough.

African fronts

Allied control of the seas prevented the Germans from supplying their colonies. A defensive strategy attempted to hold the colonies until final victory in Europe, and to draw Allied troops from the European front.

- German-Southwest Africa - A German colony, present-day Namibia. This colony was conquered from South Africa in 1915, after initial hesitation by South Africa, in less than a quarter by Commonwealth troops.
- West Africa - Germany had colonies here: today's Cameroon and Togo. Here, too, the Germans were quickly defeated, after which the colonies were divided up.
- German East Africa - present-day Tanzania, Rwanda and Burundi. On 22 August 1914 the Germans attacked with ships the Belgian port of Kalemie of Belgian Congo on Lake Tanganyika. The Germans continued to control the lake until

1916. Only a small colonial army, which was poorly equipped, was stationed in the Belgian Congo to maintain order. In 1915, Belgian army officers were trained in Le Havre for fighting in the tropics. The soldiers were recruited in Congo and the army recruited porters for supplies. There were hardly any roads.

With the aid of seaplanes and ships brought in in sections, the British and Belgian forces succeeded in gaining

La drapeau belge hissé à Tabora, le 19 septembre 1916.   De Belgische vlag te Tabora gehesen, den 19 September 1916.   The Belgian flag hoisted at Tabora, on the 19 september 1916.

Le 19 septembre 1916, entrée des troupes belges à Tabora. — Intrede van de Belgische Troepen te Tabora, den 19 September 1916.   The Belgian Troops entering at Tabora, on the 19 september 1916.

strategic control of the lake. In April 1916 the attack was launched, from the Belgian Congo by the Belgian colonial army, and from the British colonies by the British army. On 19 September 1916, the main German base at Tabora was captured.

By the end of 1917, Germany had lost all territories, but German troops continued to wage guerrilla warfare in the colony and Portuguese-Mozambique against the Portuguese and British.

This was the last place in Africa where the German colonial troops still fought. Only on 13 November 1918 news arrived here that the armistice had been signed. It was some time before the weapons were laid down

Fronts in the Middle East

- Caucasus Campaign - The Ottomans interfered in the war on the side of the Centrals. They began attacking Russia in the Caucasus and several battles were fought.
- Mesopotamian Campaign - The invasion of Iraq by troops of the British Empire.

- Palestinian Front - The British fought over Sinai and Palestine against the Ottomans, to keep the Ottomans out of the Suez Canal.

- Dardanelles Front - The Entente wanted a second route to Russia, via the Dardanelles. For this, the capital of the Ottoman Empire, Constantinople, had to be occupied. Ultimately, the Allies failed in this attack.

- Persian front - Officially Persia was an independent and neutral country but due to influence from Russia and the British Empire, oil was also fought here. Because different tribes were set against each other and to undermine the British in the Middle East and India, several more conflicts were fought here. All in all, however, not much changed.

Asian front

- Tsingtao - A few months after the start of the war, the city was captured by Japan and Great Britain at the Siege of Tsingtao. The German naval squadron, led by Admiral Maximilian von Spee, had already left for South America before then.

- Pacific Islands

The Western Front

The German General Staff started from the Schlieffen-Plan. This plan, developed by Alfred von Schlieffen, recognized the danger of a two front war against France and Russia, for which Germany was not strong enough. Therefore the plan was to bypass the French army by allowing the German army to invade the weaker defended north of France via Belgium (initially also the Netherlands).

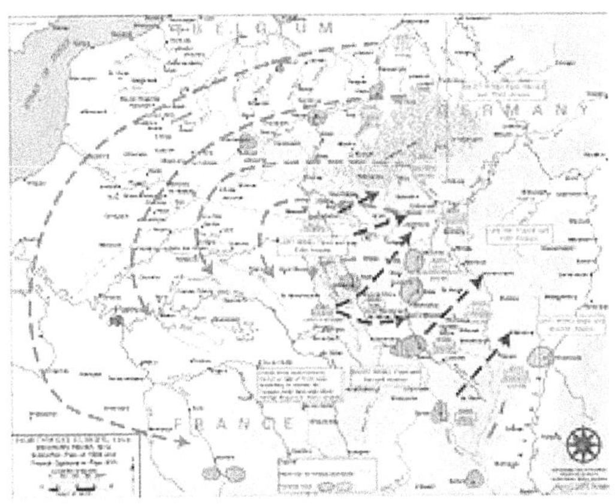

By then moving west and east around Paris - the French capital would *not be* taken - and then swinging back east, the French army concentrated in Alsace would be attacked in the rear and trapped and surrendered.

The German troops would then be put on a train to Russia to defeat the newly mobilized Russian army there. A period of only 42 days was planned for defeating the French. Thus the Schlieffen Plan.

However, the plan had weaknesses:

- By violating Belgium's neutrality, the United Kingdom might declare war on Germany under the Treaty of London of 1839. It would also deprive Germany of a lot of diplomatic credit. Von Schlieffen considered this irrelevant; after all, the plan was drawn up by military men only, not by politicians.
- A very tight schedule of 42 days was maintained. Every deviation would upset the plan. Von Schlieffen advised to negotiate with the enemy immediately after every delay: "We cannot win then anyway".
- The German army was too large for the capacities of the Belgian and Northern French (rail) road network. Moreover, the operation was probably beyond the forces of the German army. (Von Schlieffen denied this)

33

- No account was taken of the possibility that the French army would not want to surrender and would leave it to a longer confrontation.
- Also, no earlier Russian mobilization or attack was anticipated (due to the lack of industrialization in this country).
- The plan was not prepared for political situations. In the July crisis of 1914, France did not play a significant role. However, the plan foresaw French participation and the entry into force of the various alliances made France join the war. Two days before the declaration of war, France already was mobilizing and because of the dominant nationalism in France, the declaration of war was seized with great enthusiasm as an opportunity to deal with eternal enemy Germany and to regain Alsace-Lorraine. When Germany mobilized, the military implemented the plan while diplomats and politicians were passive.
- The plan assumed a war of movement, while speed of the armies of infantry and cavalry and artillery was limited.

Raid in Belgium

- **1 August 1914** - German troops invade neutral Luxembourg.
- **August 3** - Germany declares war on France and on the same day asks Belgium for permission to pass through Belgium in order to invade France. Neutral Belgium keeps its promise and offers the Germans no passage.
- **August 4** - German army units cross the Belgian border. France and the United Kingdom come to the rescue of Belgium.
- **August 6** - The German army attacks the forts around Liege.
- **August 12** - Battle of the Silver Helmets, in Halen. 140 Belgian and 160 German soldiers fall. The Belgians win and entrench at Diest.
- **15 August** - Battle of Dinant. The king and queen and the government settle in Antwerp. The king commands the army.
- **August 16** - The last fort around Liege surrenders to the Germans.
- **18 August** - Battle of the Seven Pillars, in the surroundings of Tienen, on the territory of the

present municipalities of St.-Margriete-Houtem, Grimde and Oplinter. About 2.400 Belgian soldiers faced an army of about 15.000 Germans. Half of the Belgians lost their lives or were wounded. The Belgian army retreats.

- **August 18** - King Albert I orders the Belgian army to retreat to Antwerp after a massive German attack north of the Meuse River.
- **August 19** - German reprisals in Aarschot.
- **20 August** - The Germans invade Brussels. Heavy fighting follows in Aalst, Mechelen, Dendermonde and Charleroi. In Antwerp many volunteers work day and night: trees are cut down, villas demolished, in short: everything that can obstruct the view. Shelters are erected in different places, floods near the forts from Kapellen to Kontich are carried out. In the town the Belgian, French and English flags fly. Between 21st and 24th August the Namur forts fall.
- **August 22** - Battle of Charleroi in which the French also participate. Cobblestone roads are broken throughout the country to hinder German movements.

- **On 25 August,** German troops launched a punitive expedition against the town of Louvain. 218 civilians were murdered and the town was burned to the ground. The university library also went up in flames. These unorthodox actions led to massive voluntary recruitment into the British Empire.

- **27 August** - British soldiers disembark in Ostend to reinforce the Belgian army in Antwerp. The neutral Netherlands refused to allow them to enter via the Scheldt, preventing them from disembarking in Antwerp itself. New German offensive against Mechelen with 20.000 soldiers. Later this number will be doubled. Mechelen is bombed for the first time.

- **August 30** - After three days of bombing, the forts of Walem, Sint-Katelijne-Waver and Koningshooikt are written off. They can no longer play their role of fortress to hold back the enemy, but now become support points.

- **September 2** - A zeppelin flies over Antwerp and drops seven bombs on houses set up as hospitals. 12 people are wounded and there is heavy damage.

- **5 September** - Major Von Sommerfeld orders to burn down the city of Dendermonde. Also the civil hospital and the Beguinage church from the 16th century. Houses are looted and inhabitants are deported to Germany. In Sint-Gillis and Lebbeke 25 inhabitants are killed by the passing German army.
- **September 9 to 26** - The headquarters of the Belgian armed forces are set up in Lier. King Albert stays there for several days during the Battle of the Nete.
- **September 29** - Lier is bombed, just like Duffel, Tisselt, Londerzeel and Heist-op-den-Berg. New battles for Mechelen, the Belgians have to give up Mechelen and retreat to Antwerp. On their retreat the defenders destroy the forts of Walem and Breendonk. This to prevent the Germans from using them against the Belgians.
- **October 2** - The Germans try to break through. From the balcony of the Palace on the Meir in Antwerp, King Albert I reassures the population as gunfire can be heard.
- **3 October** - Walem, Sint-Katelijne-Waver and Koningshooikt are shelled by 28 cm guns placed in

Elewijt and Hofstade. A plane scatters notes above Antwerp, calling on the population to surrender. The population laughs at this while the German plane is under fire. Further fighting in Lier. Herentals becomes the victim of German terror. Campine villages are set on fire.

- **October 4** - The front doesn't move. The Belgians are forced to entrench behind the Rupel and the Nete. Bridges are blown up. Heavy fighting in Duffel.

- **6 October** - British naval infantry brigades and the Belgian army have successfully defended the Nete. However, on the morning of October 6, they are forced to retreat to the inner fort line. As a result, the Germans can place their guns within firing range of the town. More than 4,000 shells and 140 zeppelin bombs fall on Antwerp. General Deguise announces to the population that whoever wants to leave can do so. An exodus along the Scheldt begins. More than 1 million Belgians flee to the neutral Northern Netherlands. The refugees are well received. Others go via the coast to France or try to reach Great-Britain via Ostend.

- **October 8** - To prevent the total destruction of the city of Antwerp, the Belgian and British authorities jointly decide to evacuate the city. During the night of October 8th, the King and the Queen leave Antwerp.

- **October 9** - The Battle of Antwerp is over. The forts of Schoten, Brasschaat, Merksem, Kapellen and Lillo are blown up. Under cover of night, the last Belgian division also gives up the left bank of the Scheldt and retreats to the Yser. The Antwerp city council requests and receives a cease-fire from the German supreme command. The 'Convention of Kontich' is a fact. Some 33,000 Belgian soldiers who can no longer escape move to the Netherlands and are interned there.

- **October 10** - The Belgians and British, now having left Antwerp, deal a heavy blow to the Germans as the latter try to cross the Scheldt. German units advance towards Ghent. In the north the Belgians push the Germans back to Lokeren. Near Ghent, at Melle, the Belgians were able to beat back the enemy and capture a German artillery battery. The retreat of the Belgian army takes place without major problems. All armoured trains and heavy guns are saved.

- **12 October** - The Germans occupy Ghent, which has surrendered without a struggle. The Belgian retreat continues towards the Westhoek and sets up behind the Yser.

- **13 October** - British divisions arrive at Ypres. The German army advances further all over East Flanders.

- **15 October** - The Germans advance on West-Flanders and occupy Bruges.

- **October 16** - The German army reaches Damme, Zeebrugge, Knokke and Ostend. The German 4th army positions itself at the coast up to the road Ypres - Menin. From the road Menin-Ypres the German 6th army forms the occupation force. Because of the inundation of the IJzer the front gets stuck in Flanders and later on in France. Four years of trench warfare begin, from the Belgian dunes at Nieuwpoort and De Panne to the French-Swiss border at Pfetterhouse in France.

Besides the Belgian Westhoek also the Belgian enclaves of Baarle-Hertog remain unoccupied.

These enclaves were very isolated due to the Dutch neutrality stance and had a minor role in the war by keeping a Belgian post office open for important correspondence.

The Eastern Front

Despite the 42-day mobilization period that the Schlieffen Plan allocated to the Russians, two Russian armies invaded East Prussia as early as August 1914. Units of the Russian cavalry committed numerous crimes against East Prussian civilians (the *Kosakengreuel*). At the same time, the Russians entered the Austrian province of Galicia.

The advance into Galicia was especially successful at first. After initial panic, the armies were defeated by the new commanders Paul von Hindenburg and Erich Ludendorff at

Tannenberg and the Masurian Lakes in August and September 1914. At these battles the entire Second Russian Army ceased to exist.

There were also trenches on the eastern front, but these were further apart and had the character of a temporary defence line.

There were simply not enough troops to occupy the 1200 km long front this way. The Germans used here for the first time poison gas (tear gas) against the Russians. After the battle of Lemberg, the Russians took large parts of Galicia. During winter 1914/1915 and spring, Russian and Austrian troops fought several battles in the Carpathians. The Germans then came to the aid of their Austro-Hungarian allies.

In the spring of 1915 the German general staff decided, because the western front was jammed anyway, to transfer troops to the eastern front.

At the same time, the Russian industrial base proved too narrow to provide the troops with a steady stream of clothing, food, weapons, ammunition, means of transportation, and other necessities. A major offensive of the Centrals led to a breakthrough. On August 5, Warsaw was taken.

In the middle of 1915 the Russians were driven out of Poland. Also the area which is now Lithuania and southern Latvia came into German hands. This event became known in Russia as the "Great Retreat" and in Germany as the "Great March".

The Russians organised the Broesilov Offensive against the Austrians in Galicia in 1916. This attack was initially a spectacular success, but again the Germans came to the aid of the Austrians. Romania sided with the Allies in 1916, but was nevertheless invaded and occupied by Germany, Austria and Bulgaria. The Russian offensives eventually ended with great loss of life.

The Russian war industry expanded rapidly, improving the equipment of Russian armies, but food shortages in major population centers led to unrest.

In Russia, the revolutions of 1917 followed, after which the Communists began to negotiate with the Germans.

Meanwhile, the Russian armies had disintegrated and the Germans occupied Ukraine and the area that is now northern Latvia and Estonia without a fight. The communists finally concluded the Peace of Brest-Litovsk with the Germans, which gave them a chain of vassal states and freed up the West. After the armistice these areas had to be evacuated and the Treaty of Versailles annulled the Peace of Brest-Litovsk. At the same time all the confiscated Russian and Romanian gold had to be returned.

Retaliation in Belgium

Belgium kept its agreement to remain neutral and not let the Germans through. But the German army command did not take this neutrality into account and Germany invaded Belgium after all.

On 25 August German troops murdered 218 civilians during a punitive expedition against the town of Leuven. The town was partially burned to the ground. Of the approximately 6,000 houses in Leuven, 2,117 were reduced to ashes. St. Peter's Church and the university library also went up in flames.

47

The Germans watched as a quarter of a million books, including thousands of irreplaceable medieval manuscripts and crib books, went up in flames. Besides these crimes, other similar cases created a wave of national and international outrage (later testimonies would also show that not all Germans in the field approved of these atrocities).

Leuven was not the only victim: similar atrocities were also committed in places such as Dinant (674 dead) and Aarschot (170 dead).

The German army command decided on such terrifying reprisals after their troops had, they claimed, been shot at by civilians. The argument of these so-called *francs-tireurs* was always used to justify horrendous reprisals.

Before the war began, German generals had heavily indoctrinated and stoked their own soldiers with tales of *franc-tireurs* from the Franco-German War of 1870-1871.

It was impressed upon them that during their advance they must not under any circumstances trust the local population and must act harshly if they were shot at by them.

48

This had made the German troops so paranoid that any minor incident that could not be immediately explained could give rise to such reprisals.

Public opinion was also stirred up by propaganda stories, in order to provide the army command with unconditional support for the war effort. In any case, however, no organised franc-ti riots had been ordered from above and these were probably isolated cases. Most of the reprisals were the result of misunderstandings: in Louvain, for example, the Germans appeared to have shot at each other in the confusion and in Aarschot a German colonel (who was much hated by his own men) was shot by one of his own soldiers.

A total of 500 communities were affected by atrocities during the invasion of Belgium; at least 5,000 civilians were murdered, including women and children (in northern France the number was about 1,500). It is therefore understandable that the German atrocity associated with the beginning of the invasion was an easy tool for Allied propaganda.

On both sides, crimes committed by the other side were invented or exaggerated by the propaganda, and own crimes were denied or minimized. The Germans were presented by the Allied propaganda as "Huns with pin helmets", barbarians from the East; the Belgians, on the other hand, were presented by the German propaganda as creeps who traitorously lured the German troops into ambushes.

The British Empire had guaranteed Belgium's neutrality and security by the Treaty of London. With a narrow majority in the Cabinet, it declared war on Germany. The German atrocities caused massive voluntary recruitment into the British Empire.

Massive recruitment

The British were able to draw on naive enthusiasm in their recruitment, both at home and in their colonial empire. French and German recruiters could also count on a large influx. The novel *From the Western Front No News* by Erich Maria Remarque describes the enthusiasm for war on the German side during these first few months.

And the young Adolf Hitler also stood in the midst of an enthusiastic crowd on the Odeonsplatz on 1 August 1914, when it was announced that Germany was at war.

The population still had a romanticised image of the war. There was great social pressure to fight. Recruiters spoke to them in the factories, schools, in church and on the market squares. Those who did not participate would later "no longer belong". Those who successfully evaded conscription or (as in the British Empire) did not volunteer while others did, were stigmatized as cowards. Refusers were looked down upon and given white feathers by their girls, symbols of cowardice.

It was also felt that, in exchange for the much improved social systems, one could 'give something back'. Moreover, the British army assigned men from the same neighbourhood or factory to the same army units, the so-called *pal's battalions* ('work together, fight together'). This created social pressure and social control.

Volunteers from Australia and New Zealand together formed the Anzac units. They were often given the most hopeless assignments but wore the halo of brave but reckless soldiers who zealously cultivated their image.

Young factory workers and miners from Britain were keen on a trip to Paris. In Canada, the first programmed contingent of 20,000 men was immediately filled to capacity. Another 430,000 were to follow. A total of 60,000 Canadians would die.

During the first weeks of the war, thousands of Americans from the then neutral United States reported to Canada; 5,000 of them were from Texas.

Despite the conflict between the British and the Irish with several popular uprisings, there were, besides Protestant Irish who were favourable to the British, tens of thousands of Catholic Irish who enlisted in the British professional army. Of the 200,000 Irish volunteers in the British army, about 30,000 would eventually die.

The British regarded the Irish (as well as the Scots) as "fierce warriors" who, with the "appropriate" framing by mainly English officers, could be useful in all kinds of colonial conflicts, while the Irish and Scots saw the army as a lord of the manor, who, moreover, promised "adventure" in "exotic places".

At the insistence of French government, Russia sent an expeditionary army of 8942 infantry to fight on the western front in France in 1916. Following the collapse of the Russian army and the peace agreement between Russia and Germany, many Russian ex-soldiers were put to work in the French economy; some were deported to Algeria, and some army units continued to fight or were conscripted into the French army.

The contribution of the "South Africans" was extraordinary. They had only just finished ten years of bloody war with the British and now they were allies against an enemy they only knew by hearsay. Moreover, many Boers felt akin to the colonial Germans of German South-West Africa and were reluctant to fight them.

Pro-German and militantly anti-British Afrikaners did revolt against war participation in the Maritz rebellion, but they were defeated and their leader Christiaan de Wet was arrested. British "coloured" colonial troops from India, Nepal and even Jamaica, together with the British-Chinese

Labor Corps, were conducted to Europe with dubious promises and unhampered by any imagination.

All in all, war was seen as something that would set national and international relations right, end 'social ills', purify the minds of youth, educate them and make real men of them.

Trench battle

While German policy assumed that the United Kingdom would remain neutral, the German supreme command had meanwhile prepared a war plan that would make this neutrality impossible (the Schlieffenplan). The United Kingdom guaranteed Belgian neutrality. When on 3 August this neutrality was violated and the German Uhlans set fire to the forts around Liege, London was left with no other option than to give Berlin an ultimatum and eventually declare war.

The German armies marched through Belgium and northern France. They advanced on Paris, although Paris was not the target of the attack. Meanwhile in Alsace, the French attacked according to their own Plan XVII and were beaten bloody. Masses of infantry advanced into the German trenches, where, however, they were shot down with machine guns. With their bright blue uniforms they were living targets.

The crescent-shaped advance of the Germans through Belgium and northern France initially seemed to go reasonably according to plan. Liege and the circle of giant forts surrounding it were occupied within days and the British Expeditionary Force (BEF) was defeated in the Battle of the Borders. The Germans advanced as far as the River Marne, where the French tried to hold them off. The French claimed victory but according to many historians, if there was a winner, the Battle of the Marne was won by the Germans rather than the French. However, the nervous General Staff, who had already noted minor deviations from the plan, decided to allow the German army to retreat to Chemin des Dames. The front grew by circumferential movements of both sides (the Race to the Sea) westward to the North Sea coast. The French government felt threatened in Paris and settled temporarily in Bordeaux.

57

With the exception of Spain and the Scandinavian countries, Switzerland and the Netherlands, all European countries would eventually become involved in the First World War.

It was generally expected to be a short war. Home again when the leaves fall and Back home before Christmas were common slogans. But it turned out to be an unprecedentedly long and cruel war whose fronts were fixed after only a month and a half. Already in the first months of the war in 1914 this became clear: the Belgians lost 30,000 people (in 5 months as many as in every year of the war that followed), the Germans 241,000 and the French 306,000.

What followed was a pointless trench war that cost millions of lives. One battle, like the Battle of Verdun or the Battle of the Somme, left more dead and wounded than all the battles of the previous century put together (600,000 Allied and 750,000 German casualties at the Somme).

Only very slowly did the military supreme commanders come to realize that in this war, in which they still considered the attack to be the only one, defenders always had the advantage.

Attackers died in droves because rapid fire and shell bombardments had rendered the old combat and weapons technology hopelessly outmoded.

The trench

Defense lines were formed by:

- The first line, formed by outposts, machine gun nests etc. They were connected to the main line by small trenches.
- The main line, which was the actual trench. Here the soldiers stayed and could move around.
- The hinterland. This was connected to the main line by small trenches and railways.

Between the German and Allied trenches was a strip of mud, ploughed up by shell explosions and infantry, and littered with landmines and barbed wire. The only thing that grew on the no man's land and in the trenches was the poppy. That is why this red flower is a symbol of the First World War.

Life in the trench was a nightmare. Trenches, especially in spring, winter and autumn, were muddy trenches into which one sank knee-deep in mud. Everything became damp and dirty and the water penetrated clothes and boots. This led among other things to trench feet, the soaking of long wet feet with greatly increased risk of damage and thus infections with the ultimate consequence death by gangrene.

Sometimes wooden planks were used to improve walkability; in German trenches this was somewhat more rapid. Bodies could not be buried quickly because of the circumstances and the large numbers involved. The corpses and other waste attracted rats, which multiplied rapidly. Only when a part of the front was 'at rest' for a longer period could some improvement in living conditions be achieved.

During offensives it was even worse. The defenders were sometimes exposed to artillery bombardment for days. Meanwhile, the attackers drew troops together. When (it was thought) all enemy artillery and machine gun nests were eliminated, the infantry attacked, under cover of shellfire. Sometimes the coordination was not good: then the soldiers lost their cover or were shot by their own artillery. This was also done intentionally when the infantry did not advance fast enough. Thus the soldiers crossed over the no man's land into the enemy trench.

61

However, the defenders usually already knew what was going to happen because of the intensive preparation (air reconnaissance played a major role for the first time) and days of bombing and withdrew partly.

This created a salient in which the attacking infantry got stuck. Machinegun nests on the flanks opened fire and defending infantry advanced while their own artillery was often too slow because it got stuck in the mud in the no man's land. Now completely without cover, the attacking infantry was almost entirely slaughtered, in many cases to the last man. In 1915 such smaller attacks occurred regularly.

The Germans generally had more viable trenches than the Allies. With the Allies (especially the French on whose territory the fighting took place) the construction of good trenches was discouraged from an offensive point of view and the Germans had retreated to higher and therefore more defensible (but also drier) positions.

Besides all the filth that also brought many diseases, things like continuous fear, loneliness and monotony were hell for the soldiers.

During days of shelling or during Code Red the fear of dying must have been unbearable. There are stories of soldiers who lit a cigarette and by lighting it became a target for snipers. This is the origin of the superstition that never more than one cigarette should be lit with a fire - after all, this gave snipers enough time to aim.

All the terrible and traumatic experiences in the trenches caused some soldiers to suffer from shellshock. In this condition, the soldier suffers from tics or convulsions, such as twitching of the eyes, or even shivers. Shellshock was considered a form of cowardice, so soldiers with these symptoms were usually executed by their own party.

Loneliness was common. Friendships between men rarely lasted longer than a month, partly because of the huge numbers of victims. Loneliness resulted in all sorts of strange symptoms. Some men formed friendships with rats or objects and considered them family, others talked constantly to themselves or dead bodies. The lack of women resulted in sexual relations between the men.

The monotony of a soldier's life combined with the above caused the so-called 'trench syndrome' among survivors after the war. Many men could not resume their old lives and continued to live with the same idiosyncrasies as in the trenches.

Chemical and biological warfare

In the first month of the war, August 1914, French soldiers fired tear gas (xylyl bromide) at the Germans, making them the first to use poison gas. However, the German army was the first to conduct intensive research into poison gas, led by the eminent German chemist and Nobel Prize winner Fritz Haber, and was the first to use it on a large scale in 1915. But the French, including the chemist and Nobel Prize winner Victor Grignard, were also working intensively on it.

The Germans first used xylyl bromide on the Russian front during the Battle of Warsaw, but the gas condensed due to the low temperature and even froze. Later, chlorine gas cylinders were used on a small scale on the Eastern Front for the first time.

The astonished officers saw their soldiers disappear into green clouds and fall down. Some ran back, screaming that the Germans were poisoning them with a "green fog."

After this experiment, the Germans used the gas in the Second Battle of Ypres. More than 5000 cylinders of chlorine gas were opened up. The French defending regiments were caught and a 6 km gap was created. The Germans had intended this attack as an experiment and had not counted on such a success. There were no soldiers available to push through.

After this success, various types of chemical weapons of war were created, such as phosgene and, in 1917, mustard gas. Also German and later French scientists tried to put pathogens in several bombs; especially the plague. The first steps towards serious biological warfare had been taken.

Chemical weapons were soon and widely used by the Allies. The first gas masks that appeared were primitive (for example a cloth soaked in water or urine) and hardly helped at all.

Only after extensive research the gas masks were improved considerably, which did not improve the effectiveness of the already very expensive chemical weapons. Moreover it was a very risky business for the own troops, because the wind could make the gas go the wrong way when the cylinders were opened. The latter was solved by the use of gas grenades.

Mutiny

Because of the enormous losses, not only during the big battles, but also in countless smaller battles, the French soldiers realised that simply attacking was tantamount to suicide. Yet the army command could not think of a better tactic. Many soldiers mutinied in 1917, sometimes even with whole regiments at once. In fact, mutiny is a very big word, because the soldiers did not revolt. They stopped and made passive resistance. They protested not so much against the war itself as against the tactics used, whereby soldiers were sacrificed by the thousands in attacks that achieved nothing.

The mutinous soldiers refused to carry out orders. But there was also mainly passive resistance: they laughed at officers when they read out reports of so-called victories.

As they marched to the front, they barked like sheep supposedly being led to slaughter. They frightened officers by threatening to kill them "with a stray bullet" at the next attack. They hid whenever possible to escape orders. Only those officers and non-commissioned officers who dared to live among them in the trench had any respect left.

There are no unequivocal reports on the extent of the mutiny. Official reports spoke of 2 or 'some' divisions.

According to French historians, a total of 40 to 80 thousand troops were involved, or only about 5% of the total.Historians like John Keegan, however, assume that at one point the mutiny had extended to 50 French divisions.

This panicked the Allies. If the Germans found out about this and would attack immediately, they could roll up the front from Amiens to Verdun and then walk to Paris. General Pétain, the new supreme commander, decided to talk to the soldiers.

He did this by directing loyal artillery at mutinous regiments on the one hand, but on the other hand granting better leave and not using the French army for offensives anymore. 500 French mutineers were sentenced to death in 1917, of which only 26 were effectively executed. Pétain kept his word: no more major offensives were carried out by the French army.

Belgian refugees

After the German invasion many Belgians fled. Thousands left via Ostend and Zeebrugge to England or from there to France. More than a million Belgians fled to the Netherlands. Among these refugees were also 33,000 soldiers. They were interned because, according to international law, as a neutral country the Netherlands had to ensure that troops and resources of the warring parties that landed on its territory could no longer take part in the battle. Thousands of "motivated" Belgian soldiers would escape to take part in the war via Great Britain and France.

The refugees were at first warmly welcomed. Indignation at the violation of the small country's neutrality and admiration for its fortitude were great.

However, the group of refugees was so large that problems soon arose with housing and health care. The Belgian authorities called on refugees to return to their, now occupied, homeland.

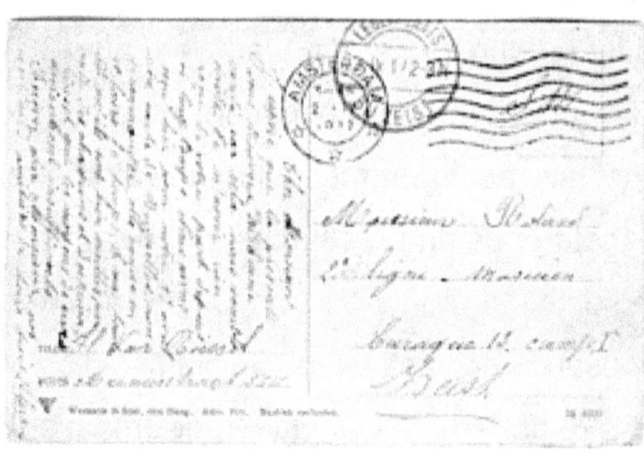

Most of the war refugees actually returned home before the end of the year. However, more than 100,000 Belgians stayed behind in the Netherlands. Among them were the families of interned military personnel. Of this group those who could not support themselves (approximately 20,000) were housed in refuges in Gouda, Uden, Nunspeet and Ede under the supervision of the Dutch government, where the Belgians were housed in very good conditions until the end of the war. Inspections by the International Red Cross, led by Switzerland, confirmed this on several occasions.

71

The refugees in the United Kingdom actually established entire Belgian colonies with all the trimmings. Typical are the Catholic churches and communities in a predominantly Protestant country. Many thousands of Belgian children took their first or solemn communion in the United Kingdom; Belgian life simply continued there.

The Belgians who had fled but were not sent to the front, set to work in their host country. In France, the dedication and zeal of the Belgians was appreciated by the factories and the farmers. Belgian maids were well regarded by the richer bourgeoisie.

Collections were made throughout the British Empire and in many neutral countries to help the Belgians. Women's organisations in Australia, New Zealand and Canada collected money and clothing for the Belgians. They baked cakes which they sold at markets, while their husbands and sons died by the dozen in Flanders. The neutral Scandinavian countries did the same, as did the North and South Americans. The Danish government, for example, paid all the costs for one of the refugee camps in the Netherlands.

After the war, the major American universities would hold a major fundraising campaign to rebuild the university library in Leuven. In May 1940, however, the Germans once again did their destructive work.

Italy

Italy yielded to the promises of the Allies. The Centrals saw this as a betrayal, since Italy, together with Austria and Germany, had the Triple Alliance. But Italy was more a burden than a support; the economically weak country had to be supplied with coal and credit by the United Kingdom, and the Italian soldiers always had to be helped by French soldiers.

Moreover, the Italians looked no further than the Austrian territories that were to become theirs. The Piedmontese resisted bravely, but the southern Italian troops lacked the motivation to fight.

Italy's battle against Austria-Hungary in World War I is also known as *the White War*. The reason is that most of the war took place in the Alps. The Italian army was commanded by the infamous marshal Luigi Cadorna.

When Italy suddenly defected to the Entente, Austria-Hungary had been at war for almost a year. Most of their army was fighting the Russians 1,200 kilometers away, in the northeastern Austrian province of Galicia. There was also another front against Serbia. Because of these war efforts, few troops were available in the Italo-Austrian border region.

There was a garrison left at the Italian border and the border had been fortified several times over the years. This was because the Austrians had always distrusted the Italians.

After the declaration of war, the troops stationed here were supplemented with reservists; people from the region who were called up in a hurry. Young men who lacked training, let alone combat experience, farmers and older men. The
75

older men (including veterans), among whom people in their fifties were no exception, could no longer be called up for military service because of their age. However, because there was an acute threat, these people were still deployed to defend the country.

Despite the composition of the army, these Austrians were well motivated and determined to keep the Italians out. Moreover, they knew the area like the back of their hand.

The Italians' only advantage was their large numerical superiority. Most of the Italian army was not motivated and also the terrain worked against the Italians. They had to take fortified mountain slopes on the Austrian side of the border. In addition, the Italian army suffered from Cadorna's incompetence and stubbornness.

When the Italians had mobilized their army, the Austrians had already entrenched themselves in the (fortified) positions on the mountainsides and peaks of the Alps (where gradients of 30-40 percent were no exception).

Because Italy wanted to take parts of the Küstenland (including Trieste) and Tyrol, Cadorna gave the order to attack the positions. Because the Infantry was not well supported by artillery (because there were too few artillery divisions) and because the Italians had a poor position in relation to the Austrians, the attacks were disastrous for the Italians. Yet Cadorna repeatedly gave the order to keep attacking, something that did not do the soldiers' already poor motivation any good.

The Italians also tried to circumvent the Austrian positions by digging tunnels in the mountains. However, the Austrians used geophones to locate the Italian tunnels. They then dug tunnels underneath the Italian ones and blew them up.

When the Austrian mountain army was supplemented with soldiers transferred from other fronts and received help from the German army, which included Erwin Rommel, things went downhill even faster for the Italian army.

The fighting was concentrated around the river Isonzo where a total of twelve battles were fought. Italian tactics consisted of closed formations that were sent towards the enemy positions. After eleven hopeless battles the morale of the Italians had fallen to an all time low.

Even compared to Allied forces on the Western Front, the equipment, rationing, training, and pay of the troops was of a dramatically low level. Cadorna's measures against falling morale, however, were counterproductive.

Among other things he reintroduced the Roman punishment of decimation and the number of executions was high. Because of this low morale the Austro-Hungarian counter-attack was particularly harsh; on 24 October 1917 Austria-Hungary, supported by the Germans, attacked in what became known as the Battle of Caporetto. Again the Germans used poison gas of similar proportions to the Verdun battle. The Italian defenses were unable to withstand such a fierce attack and had to surrender 25 kilometers. Cadorna refused to admit that a mistake had been made and the Italian High Command waited a week before issuing an order to retreat. Because of the enormous loss of men and general failure, the British and French forced Cadorna to give up his position to Armando Diaz.

It was only when Austria-Hungary finally collapsed due to internal problems that the Italians were able to occupy parts of Tyrol and Slovenia.

The large number of casualties already created a strong revolutionary atmosphere among the soldiers (mostly communist) during the war.

After the war there was great social discontent about the casualties and poor economy, it was also felt that the Allies had not kept their promises and had not allocated all the promised territories to Italy by the Treaty of Versailles. This would eventually lead to the rise of the fascists and Benito Mussolini in 1922.

The Balkans

Austria-Hungary, which had started the war against Serbia, tried to occupy it three times. Three times the Habsburgs were driven back. In 1915, after Bulgaria and Turkey joined the Central Powers, Serbia was occupied by Austria-Hungary and Bulgaria under German supervision.

Bulgaria, by the way, gave up after that. As one general said, "We have what we want (Macedonia), we do nothing more." The last Serbian and allied troops were driven to Corfu and Thessaloniki.

The latter city was surrounded by the Bulgarians. In the autumn of 1918, however, the Allies landed a large army near Thessaloniki and managed to break through and defeat Bulgaria in September 1918. In Serbia they advanced to the Danube, while British troops advanced along the coast to Istanbul.

Middle East

Before the war broke out, the Ottoman Empire had good contacts with, among others, the British and the Germans, who had helped them sporadically in the wars against the Russian Empire. The Ottoman Empire was then ruled by the triumvirate of Young Turks. However, the Russians and the British chose to work together this time.

Enver Pasha, the most influential Young Turk, had a strong preference for Germany and a great dislike for the Russian Empire, which had so humiliated the Ottoman Empire in the Balkans, Crimea and Caucasus in previous decades.

On August 2, 1914, the Turks and Germans signed a secret agreement and on November 5, the Turks declared war to the Allies. The leadership of the Ottoman Empire saw the war as the last chance to take back the territories lost to Russia around the Black Sea.

The Turks fought on four fronts. In the western part of the Empire several attacks by the British and French on the Gallipoli peninsula were successfully repelled at the Battle of Gallipoli. In the Middle East a fierce battle was fought against the United Kingdom and the nationalist Arab fighters they mobilized.

The British attacked oil-rich locations in southern Persia and Iraq several times with these armies, which consisted mainly of Muslim Indians in addition to British subjects and

Arabs, and also opened a front in Palestine, from their bases in Egypt.

The Caucasus campaign against Russia was perhaps the toughest for the Ottoman Empire; here, too, they fought over oil fields, those of Azerbaijan. In northern Persia the Ottomans, together with the Turkic-speaking peoples of Persia and with the help of German and Swedish officers, fought against the armies of the Russians and the British.

The goal of the warring parties was to secure the oil fields of Persia. The Ottoman Empire also had the objective of creating a land link to the Turkish peoples of Central Asia and China.

The Ottomans, at German insistence, declared a jihad against the Allies, trying to garner the support of the Arabs and other Muslims.

However, this had little success. The Arabs were dissatisfied with Turkish rule and were promised independence by the Allies if they would join the fight against the Turks.

83

The British, particularly Thomas Edward Lawrence ('Lawrence of Arabia'), managed to persuade Hussein ibn Ali, the Shariah of Mecca in Arabia, to fight alongside them. The Arabs and the British drove out the Turks during the so-called Arab Revolt.

On the other side of the Arabian Peninsula the British also tried to attack Turkish power by means of the Mesopotamian campaign. In 1914 the sheikh of Kuwait, formally subordinate to the Turks, defected to the British and Basra was taken. In 1915, General Charles Vere Ferrers Townshend began a steady advance towards Baghdad, but this was halted at Ctetisphon, after which Townshend and his army were besieged at Kut-al-Amara by Turkish troops led by the German Marshal Von der Goltz, and finally had to surrender in April 1916. The British saw this as a grievous defeat that had to be avenged, and in December 1916 a new force under General Frederick Stanley Maude advanced towards Baghdad.

Baghdad fell on 11 March 1917 but after that the advance stalled, at first because of strong Turkish resistance and later because of the supreme command's disinterest in this theatre of war. It was not until October 1918 that the advance was resumed, in the knowledge that an armistice was being negotiated and with the aim of occupying as much territory as possible and strengthening the negotiating position.

In two days 120 km was advanced, the Turkish army was definitively defeated, and on 14 November 1918, while the armistice had already begun, Mosul was occupied.

In the Caucasus the Turks fought against Russia with varying success. Many Armenians, one of the largest population groups in the east of the Empire, joined the Russians in the hope of founding their own national state. As a result, the Turkish military leadership had so little confidence in the Armenians during the war that they ordered the deportation of the entire Armenian population to the Syrian desert. This led to the Armenian Genocide, which claimed an estimated 500,000 to 1.5 million victims.

After the Russian Revolution, the Turkish army recaptured the Caucasus, but was forced to surrender in 1918.The Turkish government's distrust of ethnic and religious minorities also led to Greek Genocide against the Pontic Greeks, the Assyrian Genocide against the Suryoye and the great famine of the Lebanon Mountains against Druze and Maronites

After the war, the area was divided into several protectorates. France, the United Kingdom, and Russia were each given a part of the Middle East, and Turkey itself was divided up among the Greeks, Russians, Italians, Armenians, French, and British by the Treaty of Sèvres in 1920. However, the war in the Middle East continued in the form of several wars of independence, such as the Turkish War of Independence that invalidated the Treaty of Sèvres.

Africa and Asia

Germany's modest colonial empire was dismantled relatively easily. Everywhere the Germans were numerically far outnumbered and cut off from their homeland. German Togoland, Cameroon and German Southwest Africa had already been occupied by the Allies in 1914 and early 1915.

An army of 60,000 Japanese surrounded the small German garrison of Kiautschou. Several Pacific islands were also occupied by the Japanese, while the British occupied Emperor Wilhelmsland and the Solomon Islands from Australia.

China declared war on Germany and sent thousands of workers to the trenches for support work.

Japan did not send a man to the front after occupying the German colonies and concessions, but did issue an ultimatum to China (the Allies, by the way, whistled back at Japan). Assigning the German concessions in China to archenemy Japan was particularly resented by Woodrow Wilson by the Chinese, and also by many Americans.

87

Only in German East Africa, later Tanzania, did the Germans, led by Paul von Lettow-Vorbeck, hold out until after the armistice of 1918.

The air war

Initially, air warfare played a modest role. Aircraft were, as in the Balkan wars, only used for reconnaissance flights. The first air battle took place in August 1914 when a Serbian reconnaissance aircraft encountered an Austro-Hungarian aircraft. The pilot drew a revolver and shot at the Serbian aircraft. Immediately all pilots were equipped with revolvers, later followed by airborne machine guns.

Reconnaissance was and remained the main purpose of the aircraft. Bombing raids also occurred, but for this the pilot had to keep the bomb between his legs and work out the plane himself. Also zeppelins were used. These behemoths could carry more bombs and were often used by the Germans to bomb London.

However, they were also an easy target and very vulnerable because they were so large and filled with hydrogen. In addition to reconnaissance and bombing, intimidation of the population was a goal of the use of aircraft and zeppelins.

Known were the many "dogfights" between the German and Allied pilots.

Manfred von Richthofen, or the Red Baron, achieved 80 victories. The Frenchman René Fonck was not far behind with 75. Hermann Göring, later air marshal and Nazi Party president, was also a war pilot.

American war participation

Germany answered the Allied blockade with the submarine weapon. German submarines scoured the seas and torpedoed merchant ships. In addition to Allied ships, neutral ships such as the Lusitania were sometimes hit.

This was blamed on the Germans by many neutrals, including the United States. However, the Americans long kept their distance from the war, which they saw as a European affair, because of the Monroe Doctrine.

In 1917 there was no movement on the fronts. A German attempt to destroy the British fleet to break the blockade had failed in 1916 with the naval battle of Jutland.

The Germans destroyed more ships than the British, but no longer ventured into the open sea. Unlimited submarine warfare would provide the opportunity to isolate and force the United Kingdom to surrender. However, this could lead to a war with the United States.

The Germans continued the plan, but tried to have Japan and Mexico join the Centrals in order to distract the Americans. A telegram with this meaning (Zimmermann-telegram) was intercepted by the British secret service and handed over to the American government.

In response to this, and to the unrestricted submarine war, President Woodrow Wilson, on Allied hands from the start, was able to persuade the U.S. House of Representatives to declare war on Germany on April 6, 1917.

The Mexicans had finished the Mexican Revolution and had no need for another battle. Japan had no need to change sides.

The American presence, especially in the beginning, had a purely psychological value. As colossal as the U.S. Navy was, their land army was small. There was plenty of manpower, but insufficient armament. Cannons had to be borrowed from the British.

However, the Germans faced a new army that was growing all the time. Their submarines were insufficient to stop the war convoys. Time worked to their disadvantage: more and more troops streamed into Europe and the intact American arms factories were operating at full capacity. The Battle of the Scheldt was fought with an important deployment of American ground troops. The Flanders Field

American Cemetery and Memorial is a silent witness to this.

List of the most important battles on the Western Front

- Battle of the Borders
- Forts around Liege
- Battle of Halen, Battle of the Silver Helmets
- Fortresses of Antwerp
- First Battle of Bergen
- Second Battle of Bergen
- Battle of the Yser
- Battle of Ypres
    - First Battle of Ypres
    - Second Battle of Ypres
    - Third Battle of Ypres
    - Fourth Battle of Ypres, Lys Offensive
- The mine battle in Messines
- Battle of Passchendaele
- Battle of the Marne
- Chemin des Dames
- Battle of Verdun
- Fort Douaumont
- Battle of the Somme

* Battle of Cambrai

* Hindenburg Line

* Kaiserschlacht

* Battle of the Scheldt

Other important battles:

* Battle of Neuve-Chapelle

* Battle of Artois

* Battle in the Champagne region

* Battle of Loos

* Battle of Nivelle

* Battle of Arras

* The battle of Amiens

The Spanish flu

In 1918 a wave of flu spread around the world. Its existence became known through the Spanish media which began to report on a flu wave in which people were dying.

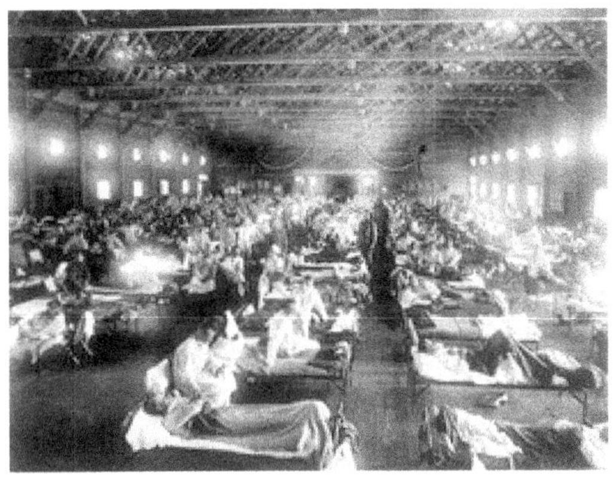

Because of this, the flu was soon known as the Spanish flu. This flu wave turned out to come from the American troops that had been sent to Europe. The Americans also infected other army corps: the British, the French, and eventually the Germans. When the troops returned after the war, the flu spread through the festive parades welcoming the troops.

Unlike most diseases, the Spanish flu not only killed small children and the elderly, but also people between the ages of 20 and 40.

Moreover, the resistance of many people had been undermined. Conservative estimates assume that this pandemic caused 20 million deaths, higher estimates go up to 100 million. If one counts these victims as deaths caused by World War I, the total death toll exceeds that of World War II, making it the deadliest conflict humanity has ever known.

Conscientious Objectors

There were also those who refused to serve out of conscientious objection.

In the Netherlands, for example, there was the Dienstweigeringsmanifesto 1915 and in the United States conscientious objectors were "conscientious objectors".

These included the "Hutterite" brothers Jacob, Michel and David Hofer and their brother-in-law Jacob Wipf, the Roman Catholic Ben Salmon (who was also condemned by his own American church), Roger Baldwin (who founded the American Civil Liberties Union).

They were locked up and some died - neglected and mistreated - in captivity. The health of many was found to be impaired after release.

The end of the war

After the peace with Russia, German troops were brought from the Eastern Front to the West, insofar as they were not used as occupation.

About half a million soldiers returned from the East. In the summer of 1918 German generals Paul von Hindenburg and Erich Ludendorff decided to go all out with these troops one more time. The Germans attacked on the western front at three points:

1. An offensive on the Marne against the French (Operation *Blücher-Yorck*);

2. An offensive on the Somme to drive a wedge between the French and British (Operation *Michael*);

3. An offensive against the British and Belgians at Ypres in Flanders (Operation *Georgette*).

At first sight, the offensives on the western front were successful: the trenches were abandoned and the Centrals gained a lot of ground, they were 50 kilometers from Paris.

Also the Germans together with Austrian troops started a successful offensive against Italy in the Alps. The Italian troops were driven back hundreds of miles into their own country. The Italian army command was dismissed and the already low morale among the Italian troops was completely broken.

However, the offensives ran aground after a while. Although the Italians were unable to offer any significant resistance, by the end of the summer the Austrian army was war-weary and could no longer advance into Italy under its own power. The German offensive on the western front also stalled in another trench battle.

The Allies took over the initiative and decided in autumn to open a third front where they saw the best chances for victory. An overwhelmingly large army of 900,000 Allied soldiers landed in the Greek coastal city of Thessaloniki, with the aim of attacking Centrals ally Bulgaria.

Thus, neutral Greece was dragged into the war, but with the consent of the Greeks themselves: after the war they would get a part of Bulgaria. Also, the Allies launched an immense offensive to the West, with the help of the newly arrived Americans, against Germany. Under the influence of this offensive, combined with other events and a German revolution, the Allies would eventually win the war.

The Fall of the Centrals in the autumn of 1918 came quickly. After some battles, Bulgaria was defeated and signed an armistice on September 29, 1918. The revolt of the Arabs against the Ottoman Empire also brought internal division and the Ottomans capitulated to the French and British on October 30, 1918. The British and French divided the Middle East.

It is a fallacy to think that the Allies were making strong war efforts against Austria-Hungary. Italy had never been a

101

strong party, but its army was now completely overwhelmed. There were other issues at play in Austria-Hungary: the country itself was war-weary and there were internal divisions. Slavic nationalism played an increasing role in the Habsburg monarchy towards the end of the war. On 18 October 1918 Czechoslovakia declared independence. This was followed by various Slavic minorities (Croats, Serbs, Bosnians) and finally even Hungary denounced the Dual Monarchy with Austria.

They asked the Italians for a truce, but they refused. The Italian army saw its chance and quickly recaptured the previously lost territories and drove the Austrians further and further back. Their goal was the city of Trieste on the Adriatic coast.

After the war ended, the Italians were granted several regions, including the German-speaking South Tyrol. But the Italians felt that they had been given too little during the negotiations in the French Versailles. The Italian negotiator Orlando even walked out of the negotiations angry. Fascism was soon born in Italy and in the 1920s Mussolini came to power.

With the fall of Austria-Hungary German generals Hindenburg and Ludendorff knew it was over. Morale in the German army plummeted to an all-time low, especially as the Allies had agreed with the Austrians that troops could be moved freely across their territory: the entire German southern border was under threat of invasion by the Allies.

In addition, the German offensives had stalled a month or two earlier and the current situation offered no prospect of victory. The German armies finally lacked everything and revolution was imminent. Through General Wilhelm Groener, they informed the emperor that they could no longer count on the loyalty of the German army. A stiffening of resistance in Flanders was only apparent: there was a shortage of everything, even uniforms. The Germans began to withdraw from Belgium and eventually even gave up territories which had been occupied for four years. The Allies gained immense ground.

The German naval leadership planned a last battle against the British fleet: even though there was nothing more to be gained. But the sailors and marines involved knew by now that this was totally pointless and no longer felt the need to risk their lives for a lost war.

A rebellion of sailors in the northern German ports broke out and spread to the whole country. The German revolution had been declared in early November 1918, eventually abolishing the monarchy and proclaiming the German republic; the Kaiser fled to the Netherlands where he died in 1941.

Negotiations, conducted by civilians, took place, and an armistice was agreed upon. The armistice was signed on November 11th 1918, at 5 am by the French commander Ferdinand Foch and the German delegation, but it did not come into effect until 11 am. During these last six hours many casualties fell on both sides, while the surrender was already signed. That the surrender was signed by civilians and not by military authorities is very important: the Nazis later exploited this fact by blaming the defeat on "a stab in the back of the troops by red elements". This story would remain in circulation as the dagger thrust legend.

The Treaty of Versailles followed in 1919.

Consequences

In addition to the immediate damage, the war had a large number of political, economic and social consequences. The world before the 'Great War' had disappeared forever. The centuries-long global supremacy of Europe was over. The 19th century optimistic belief in progress had made way for cultural pessimism.

Victims

A direct consequence of the fighting was, of course, the destruction of the lives of many people in the areas concerned. Millions of young men (in the warring states a large part of the 16 to 30 year old generation) had lost their lives as conscripts or volunteers, many had been maimed for life and millions of civilians had become refugees. The map below shows the number of soldiers per belligerent country and the number of casualties. The numbers for England include the areas that were part of the British Empire at that time.

In addition, millions of animals (horses, donkeys, but also elephants, dogs and homing pigeons) died in the First World War, which were used for transport and communication, among other things: there were relatively few cars. In 2004 the Animals in War Memorial was erected in Hyde Park in London.

World War I thoroughly shuffled the maps of both Europe and the world. New states emerged in Europe and the Middle East.

Countless international conflicts would arise from the new borders. In Russia, communism had come to power and the Soviet Union was born. Poland regained its independence and the Baltic States were founded.

The German Empire was replaced by the shaky Weimar Republic. The Austro-Hungarian Dual Monarchy had disappeared. The Balkans fell apart into separate states, including the Kingdom of Serbs, Croats and Slovenes (renamed the Kingdom of Yugoslavia in 1929). The Ottoman Empire gave way to the Republic of Turkey. Palestine was occupied by the British and became a British Mandate in 1922. A single war thus put an end to four age-old dynastic empires: the Romanovs (1917), the Habsburgs (1918), the Hohenzollerns (1918) and the Ottomans (1923). Europe had been weakened by the war.

Later, after the Second World War, the Soviet Union and the United States would take charge of the most severely affected states.

Economic and social impact

In addition to the direct damage, the economic damage was also enormous. Countries like France, Germany, Italy and Great Britain had to contend with an enormous debt burden, while especially in the former combat zones many factories etc. lay in ruins.

Also the neutral countries suffered from the war. In the Netherlands there was a coal shortage so the train service had to be reduced and the train fares were raised to limit the transport. Trade by sea was hampered, causing all kinds of shortages. In the Netherlands civilians were called to arms to strengthen the army.

The "innocent Enlightened Europe" of the 19th century was gone. States came down hard on each other. Customs tariffs were introduced or increased, and in the 1930s countries devalued their currencies without consulting other countries.

Not cooperation, but distrust and antagonism was the motto. This exacerbated the Great Crisis that lasted from 1929 to the 1930s. Besides at the state level, this also had its effect at the level of the "common man".

Authoritarian ideologies such as communism and fascism emerged. These were fueled in part by embittered veterans who were psychologically dislocated by their experiences and no longer fit into society (especially in the losing countries, which were further affected by overly harsh peace treaties).

They found refuge in various squads that were affiliated with political movements. Examples were the SA, Fasci di Combattimento, Pijlkruisers, the Iron Guard, and the commando squads of the KPD (Kommunistische Partei Deutschlands). Moderates were caught between these two fires of violence. In many countries, democracy was replaced by authoritarianism.

The thugs, made up of embittered veterans, got into fights with each other, with moderates, or with anyone whose face they didn't like, it didn't matter. Some historians see here a cause for the "brutalisation" of society ("senseless violence").

Workers and soldiers from colonies became "infected" with nationalism and communism. The "superior whites" used the resources of the colonies to beat each other up. The seeds for the later liberation movements such as Vietminh and PKI were sown.

The Allies imposed very hard peace conditions upon the Centrals. Borders were drawn quite arbitrarily, with political interests prevailing over those of the people who happened to live there.

In addition to streams of refugees, the treaties also produced latent feelings of hatred and revenge. The Second World War would give expression to these feelings. The concept of "total war" was born.

110

Trade unions were rewarded for their support of the war with recognition. The same applied to the combatants in terms of voting rights: universal single vote (one man, one vote) and (later) women's suffrage were introduced.

Women should have filled the open places in factories and workshops. This gave them a freedom they had never had before. They realised that they could do a lot of men's work themselves and gained more self-confidence.

Women did not give up their position after the war, which gave feminism an enormous boost. In Belgium, the war also exposed linguistic abuses. French-speaking officers (behind the front) gave orders to Flemish soldiers at the front.

However, several soldiers were punished for being Flemish. For example, 10 front soldiers were banished to a disciplinary company in Orne, Normandy. Known as *Orne lumberjacks,* they had to perform forced labour in very difficult living conditions.

It was a war that began with the military tactics of the Franco-German War of 1870. With cavalry charges, massive infantry deployments and bayonet attacks that
111

were as massive as they were futile. On the French side this tactic was practiced to the full. The name for this tactic (called *Elan*) of attacking with large groups of infantry in an offensive form was: *Offensive à Outrance* (*attack to the extreme*).

It was also a war that would end with the tactics of World War II: in this war, tanks and planes took part in combat for the first time. But above all, it was the war that would wipe out an entire generation of Europeans.

In total, almost nine million soldiers and one million civilians were killed in action. In addition, nearly six million civilians died of starvation and disease.

Kaiser Wilhelm II wrote after the war in his place of exile Doorn in his *Kriegserinnerungen*:

> *"When I think back to those difficult four years of war with their heaps and defeats, with their brilliant triumphs and their losses of precious blood, a feeling of fervent thanks and of imperishable admiration for the matchless deeds of the German people in arms glows within me...."*

www.ingramcontent.com/pod-product-compliance
Lightning Source LLC
Chambersburg PA
CBHW070540160726
48003CB00004B/1823